THE

WONDER THAT IS YOU

CHARLES GRAMET

ILLUSTRATED BY WILLIAM BURNARD

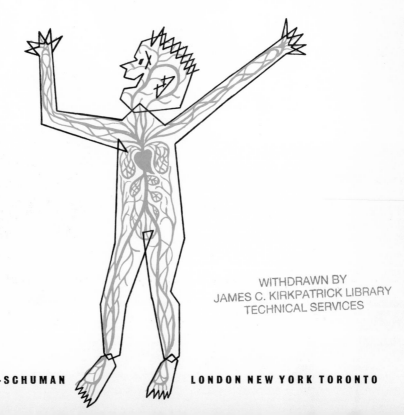

ABELARD-SCHUMAN   LONDON NEW YORK TORONTO

JE
612
G76

THE GREATEST WONDER

Of all the wonders you know, which would you say is the greatest wonder?

Atomic engines, jet planes, rockets, television?

Do you know that:

No machine can build itself. You build yourself.
No machine can repair itself. You repair yourself.
No machine can think. You can think for yourself.
No machine can make others like itself. You will be able to do so.

Boys and girls are the greatest wonders. Do you wonder what makes you such wonders? You will learn the answers in this book.

LIVING ENGINES

"Where do you get so much energy?"

You have heard that before, haven't you? Boys and girls are full of it.

You use energy when you walk, run, jump a rope, or ride a bike. You use energy when you throw a ball or carry a bag of books. You use energy when you talk, sing, or shout.

Play is really happy work.

Energy is the power to work. You need energy to play, too.

An automobile gets energy from its engine. The engine is the power plant of the car. Energy from the engine is used in many parts of the car.

Energy drives the wheels. It pumps gasoline, oil, and water. It heats the car.

muscle under microscope   muscle cells   blood cells   nerve cells

You do not have one engine that supplies energy to all parts of your body. You have thirty trillion engines.

Your body is made up of many tiny parts, like the bricks of a building. But each of your tiny parts is alive!

The tiny parts of your body are called cells. And each cell is its own engine.

Engines obtain energy from fuels. An automobile engine uses gasoline as a fuel. Your cell engines get energy from the food that you eat.

Gasoline is a fuel. Food is a fuel.

A fuel must be burned to give up its energy. In an automobile engine the gasoline is mixed with air. A spark explodes it.

Energy is given off when the mixture of gasoline and air explodes. This energy runs the car. And the engine gets very hot.

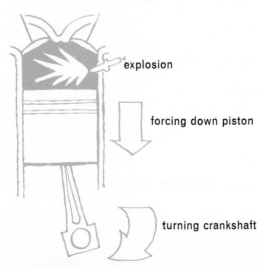

explosion

forcing down piston

turning crankshaft

9

It does not work so simply in your cell engines. You could not have food exploding in your body. And you could not stand so much heat.

But you do get warm when you play. This tells you that your cell engines are working.

Some cell engines do more work than others. For example, your muscle cells use more energy than your brain cells. Brain work does not need so much energy.

Whenever a fuel is burned, air is used and the same wastes are left. These wastes are water and a gas called carbon dioxide.

Besides, much heat is given off.

You get these wastes when coal, oil, or gas is burned in a stove. You find them in the smoke that comes from an automobile engine.

And you can find them in your breath! You can prove this to yourself.

Breathe close to a window. Does it become wet from the water in your breath? It does.

Ask your mother to show you how to take your temperature with a thermometer. You find that the inside of your body is warmer than the air in the room. Your cell engines give off heat.

If your teacher has a little lime water (calcium hydroxide) in the laboratory put a little in a glass. Breathe into it through a straw. Does the lime water turn milky? It does. It always does when carbon dioxide mixes with it.

And so your cell engines supply you with energy to play and work, and heat to keep you warm.

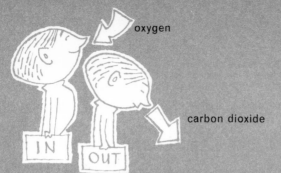

oxygen

carbon dioxide

IN

OUT

SUPPLYING AIR TO THE BODY ENGINES

A fire dies quickly if it does not get air. An automobile engine will not explode its gasoline if it does not get air.

And your cell engines will not supply you with energy if you do not supply them with fresh air.

Your chest pumps air into and out of your body. The power to pump comes from your chest muscles. It comes, also, from a strong muscle inside your body.

When these muscles tighten, the chest becomes larger. This draws air in through your nose.

When these muscles slacken, the chest becomes smaller. Then used air is pushed out of the body.

This is breathing.

Put your hands on the sides of your chest as you breathe. Do you feel your chest become larger and smaller?

Count the number of times that you breathe in a minute while you sit quietly. Then get up and jump up and down a few times. Now count again the number of times that you breathe in a minute.

While you sit quietly you breathe between 18 and 24 times a minute. After hard play you breathe very much faster. Can you tell why?

You can work it out. You must get more air to the cell engines to get more energy. Faster breathing supplies fresh air faster to the cell engines.

About one fifth of the air that you breathe in is a gas called oxygen. There is almost no carbon dioxide in fresh air.

11

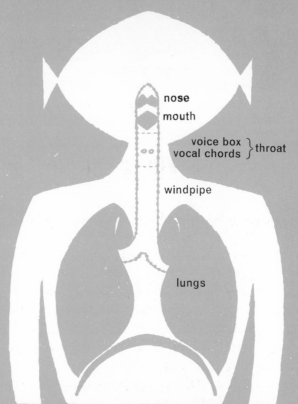

nose

mouth

voice box } throat
vocal chords

windpipe

lungs

The air that you breathe out has less oxygen in it. But now there is carbon dioxide in it. The amount of carbon dioxide that has been added to it is nearly equal to the amount of oxygen that has been removed from it.

This must mean that some of the oxygen in the air is used by the cell engines to get energy from fuel.

Oxygen is needed for burning. Oxygen is needed to obtain energy from food. Fresh air has more oxygen in it than used air has. Carbon dioxide is the waste from burning fuel.

As the air passes through the nose on the way in, it is warmed and cleaned.

The air goes to the lungs through air pipes. The opening into these pipes is in the throat.

From the throat the air goes first into a thick windpipe. This branches many times, like the branches of a tree.

Very small branches of the windpipe bring air to the lungs. Your lungs are not hollow bags, like balloons. A lung is more like a large bunch of very tiny grapes.

At the end of each of the smallest air pipes there is a very tiny bag. It is called an air sac. There are ever so many of them in each lung.

Each air sac has a network of very thin blood tubes called capillaries around it. Oxygen passes from the air sac into the blood as it flows through this network.

Blood carries oxygen to the cell engines.

Blood carries the waste carbon dioxide from the cell engines back to the air sacs. Here the carbon dioxide passes from the blood into the air sac. Breathing out gets it out of the body.

Each cell is such a tiny engine. But all the cell engines work well together to supply your energy needs for play and for work.

The cell engines repair themselves. They even replace themselves when they wear out. They are quite wonderful engines.

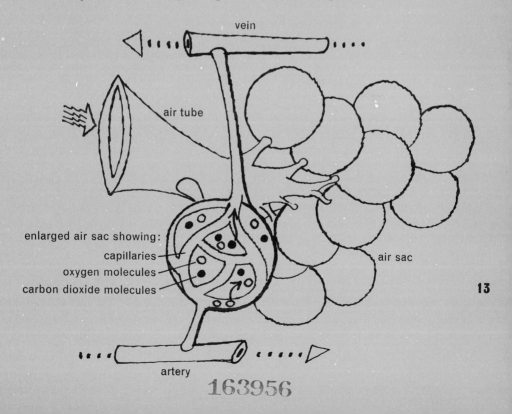

vein

air tube

enlarged air sac showing:

capillaries

oxygen molecules

carbon dioxide molecules

air sac

artery

13

SUPPLYING FUEL TO THE BODY ENGINES

You don't have to be called for dinner, do you? Your stomach tells you that it is time to eat. Hunger is the signal.

You use a lot of energy when you play. Hunger is the signal that tells you it's time to replace the fuel that has been used up. You do so when you eat.

What foods give you the most energy? You may have Dad or Mother help you make this test.

Take a small piece of cold, hard butter. Shape it like a candle. Place it in a dish. Put a wick of thin cord in the middle of it. Light it.

Will the candle burn? It will.

A food that burns easily is a good fuel. Butter is a good fuel food.

Which of the foods you eat are good fuel foods? The best are the fatty foods. The list includes many that you like very much and eat often.

You get a lot of energy from butter, cream, cheese, bacon, lamb chops, steak, hamburgers, and eggs. You may add ice cream and nuts to this list.

These are rather high-priced foods. There are many that are less costly. And the body can use them more easily than fatty foods.

You wouldn't make a meal of any one of the fatty foods in the list. You would surely add potatoes, or peas, or beans, some bread or rolls.

These have starch in them. Starch is a good fuel for the body, but only about half as good as fat.

The cereals that you eat for breakfast are all good, starchy foods. The list includes oatmeal, cracked wheat or corn, rice and tapioca, and all the other dry cereals which come ready to eat in boxes.

Sweet foods that have sugar in them are like starchy foods as fuels. For your sweet tooth, and for fuel, you may eat cakes and pies, jams and jellies, honey and sugar for sweetening. And, of course, sweets and candy.

Because they like the taste so well, boys and girls often eat too much sweet food. If you do so between meals, it may spoil your appetite for other foods that you need. And you may eat more sweets than are good for you.

You should eat enough fuel foods to supply all your needs for energy. But if you eat much more than you need, it piles up in the body as fat. You know boys or girls who are called "chubby", or "fatty", or even "fatso".

It is a bad habit to eat more than you need. You don't look well, you don't work or play as well.

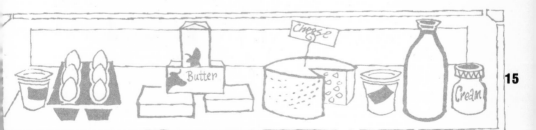

FOOD FOR THE GROWTH OF CELLS

Your cell engines need more than fuel.

How often have you heard this? "My, how you have grown!"

You grow when you add to the number or to the size of your cells. To grow you must have more of the material of which cells are made.

Cells are made of a very special material. It is called protoplasm. You should learn this word at once. It is the name of the most important material on this earth.

Protoplasm is living material.

Your cells make protoplasm from the materials that you eat. They use these materials to repair themselves as well as to grow larger, and to make new cells.

No scientist has been able to make living material from non-living material. How cells can do so is one of the great mysteries of life.

The materials for cell growth come from foods like these: lean meats, poultry, fish, eggs, oatmeal, peas, bread.

All these foods have a lot of protein in them. Proteins are used to make protoplasm.

Besides protein you need minerals to make protoplasm. Iron and lime are minerals, for example. There are a few others that you need.

You don't have to eat nails to get iron, or limestone to get lime. A little, enough, is found in many of the foods that you eat.

Minerals have other uses in your body. You use them to build strong bones and teeth and for making red blood. They help, too, to make your muscles strong.

You will get enough of all the minerals you need when you eat your cereals, meat (fish once in a while), green and yellow vegetables, and milk.

More than half of your protoplasm is water. So, you must have water, too, to make protoplasm.

Most foods have a lot of water in them. A large glass of milk with each meal will supply a good part of the water that you need in a day. You should drink a few glasses of plain water each day between meals.

You use water too, in your body, to make blood and to make juices that your body needs. And water helps to clean out wastes from your body.

THE VITAMIN FRIENDS

Peppy Pete [Vit B]   Sunshine Sue [Vit D]   Citrous Sam [Vit C]   Sharp-eyed Sheila [Vit A]

Some boys and girls like to fill up on meat and potatoes and leave their vegetables on the plate. Then their cells miss something that they need to work well, grow well, keep healthy.

They miss vitamins. These are food stuffs that help you grow well, that help you get energy, that protect you against some sicknesses.

You will get enough of the different vitamins that you need if you eat like this:

Eat plenty of milk, cheese, and butter to grow good teeth and straight bones.

Carrots and greens, eggs, and liver will help you see better at night. And your skin will be soft and smooth.

Eat plenty of bread, cereals, and greens for a good appetite and lots of energy.

Meat, liver, and milk will give you good, red blood, will help you grow strong and straight, and keep you calm.

You see that if you eat all the different kinds of foods that are set before you, you will get all your vitamins. You will have all the energy you need for play. You will feel better, you will look better. And you won't need a lot of pills.

Now that you know what to eat, how much should you eat? You have a built-in control—your appetite.

The trouble is that some boys and girls do not obey when their appetites say, "Enough". That's how they get fat.

Fat is not real growth. It is just stuffing. It doesn't make you strong or give you more energy. It really slows you down. And you don't look as well.

You may be sure that Mother gives you enough to eat at meal-time. It is the extra helpings and the many snacks between meals that add the fat.

You will look better, feel better, play better, if you stop when your appetite says you have had enough for your body needs.

YOUR FOOD MILL

The next time you go to a supermarket, look at the corn foods. You will find corn flakes, corn meal, corn starch, corn syrup, and corn oil.

The corn-on-the-cob has gone through a mill. It has been changed so that it may be used more easily in a number of ways.

The food that you eat also goes through a mill, your food mill.

Suppose you take a bite of a meat sandwich. Your mouthful will have a small piece of meat, a piece of bread, butter. What happens to them in your food mill?

Your front teeth bite off a mouth-size piece. Then your crusher teeth or molars get to work on it. Your tongue and cheeks keep pushing the food between your teeth.

At the same time the food is mixed with saliva. This is a juice that is made in your mouth.

The food becomes crushed, soft, and wet. It is more easily swallowed when it is so.

Besides, the saliva changes the food. You can find out how the food is changed.

Chew a piece of bread or a plain cracker biscuit that is not sweet. Make sure that it is well mixed with saliva. Keep it in the mouth for a while.

Does it taste sweet after a while? Saliva changes some of the starch in the cracker into sugar.

From the mouth the food passes to your throat. You remember that the windpipe starts in the throat. So does the short food tube, or gullet.

If you talk while you swallow, the food may get into the wrong pipe. If it gets into the windpipe you will cough until you get the food out.

19

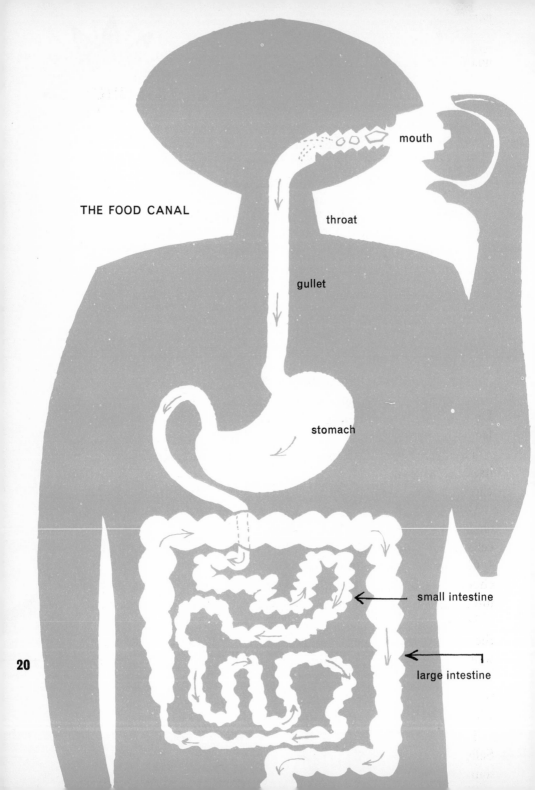

THE FOOD CANAL

mouth

throat

gullet

stomach

small intestine

large intestine

20

If you swallow without talking, and without hurry, a cover closes over the windpipe. Then the food goes into the right pipe, the gullet.

The food doesn't drop through the gullet. It is pushed down by muscles. Even if you stood on your head while eating, the food would still be pushed along to the stomach.

In the stomach, for about four hours, the food is really beaten up. It is tossed, tumbled, shaken and squeezed by the strong stomach muscles. At the end it looks like a thick pea soup.

The food is mixed with a juice that is made in the wall of the stomach. The protein bits from the meat and from the bread are changed by the stomach juice into very much smaller and simpler bits.

At the end of the stomach the muscles are closed tightly. This keeps the food in the stomach. Every once in a while the muscles slacken. Then some of the soupy stuff passes into the next part of the food mill.

Now the food starts a long journey, about twenty feet long, through the long, narrow food tube, the intestines. The inside feels like fur. There are ever so many tiny fingers, each as thin as a hair.

The food is sqeezed and pushed along by muscles in the wall of the tube. It is mixed with three different juices.

The milling and changing of the food that you ate is completed in the long, narrow food tube. It no longer looks anything like the food that you ate. And the juices have changed it into other materials.

Why must the food be milled and changed? You may be sure that you are not made of meat, and bread, and butter and the many other foods that you eat.

Your body breaks up the food to get from it the materials it needs to make protoplasm, to use as fuel, to make juices and other body materials.

Besides, the smallest bits of meat, and bread, and butter are still too large to get into the blood to be carried around the body to all the cells.

Foods must be broken down into very, very tiny bits of simple stuffs. This is called digestion. Then they can pass into the blood to be carried to the cells. And the cells can then use them for energy, for growth, and to make the other materials that your body needs to keep you alive, active, and healthy.

The simple stuffs of the broken down, digested, changed food pass into the blood that flows in the walls of the long intestine. The blood flows through the tiny, hairlike fingers that make up the wall of the tube.

The blood from the long, narrow intestine will flow to all parts of the body. And all your cells will be supplied with the materials that they need, from the food you ate.

Not all of the food can be changed in this way. What cannot be changed, what is left, is waste. It is pushed by muscles into the wide food tube or large intestine.

The food waste is stored here for twelve or more hours. Once or twice a day it is let out of the body.

The journey of the meat, bread, and butter (or what is left of them) through the whole length of the food mill takes almost a full day. Since you take in food at least three times a day, your food mill is kept busy.

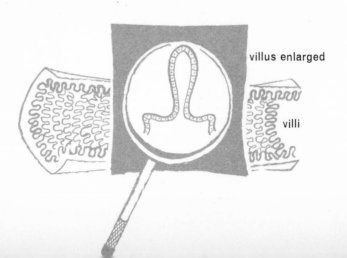

villus enlarged

villi

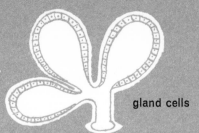
gland cells

YOUR CHEMICAL FACTORIES

Do you know that you own some very wonderful chemical factories? They are inside you. They are called glands.

The workers in your gland factories are cells. Each gland has its own kind of workers. They make its special kind of chemical or chemicals.

We have no idea how the cells are able to make all the different chemicals that your body needs. It is another of the mysteries of cells.

Glands use stuffs from the food that you eat to make their chemicals. The blood absorbs these stuffs in the long, narrow intestine, as you know, and brings them to the glands.

Some glands are very small factories, just single cells. But then there are very many of them. Such single glands are found in the wall of your stomach and of your long, narrow intestine.

Other glands have very many cells, like factories with many workers. The chemicals come out of these glands through tubes which bring them to the places where they will be used.

The glands that make saliva, for example, are such glands. Saliva is brought to the mouth. Here, as you know, it changes some starch to sugar.

Chemicals that change food are called enzymes.

Enzymes are very important chemicals. Your body makes ten different kinds just to change the food that you eat. The cells themselves make an enzyme to help them obtain energy from their fuel.

23

The glands that make enzymes that change food usually begin to work when food enters the food mill. But you can turn them on without eating, like this.

Think very hard of some foods that you would like very much, right now.

How about a nice juicy piece of steak, with mashed potatoes and green peas? After that, would you like ice cream or chocolate pudding?

Is your mouth watering? Is it full of saliva? Thinking about food can start the glands in your mouth working.

Sometimes you come into the house and smell something cooking, or baking or roasting. Your mouth begins to water.

Or you are seated at the table. Mother brings in the food and sets it on the table. You are polite and you wait to be served. But your mouth waters even before the food is set before you.

When you put the food into your mouth your tongue tastes it. Then the saliva flows very freely. And the juices begin to flow throughout the food tubes.

Smelling, seeing, tasting, even thinking about food can start the glands working. And you have juices ready to work on the food as it moves along the food tubes.

Every working cell makes some enzymes.

You remember that fuel burns quickly in a stove. And it explodes in an automobile engine. There are flames and very much heat is given off.

Your body could not stand such burning. The cells make enzymes that obtain energy from the fuel without real burning. And only a little heat is given off. Your cells are quite wonderful engines!

You have, also, glands of a very different kind. They make very different kinds of chemicals. We call them "control chemicals" or hormones.

THE HORMONE GLANDS

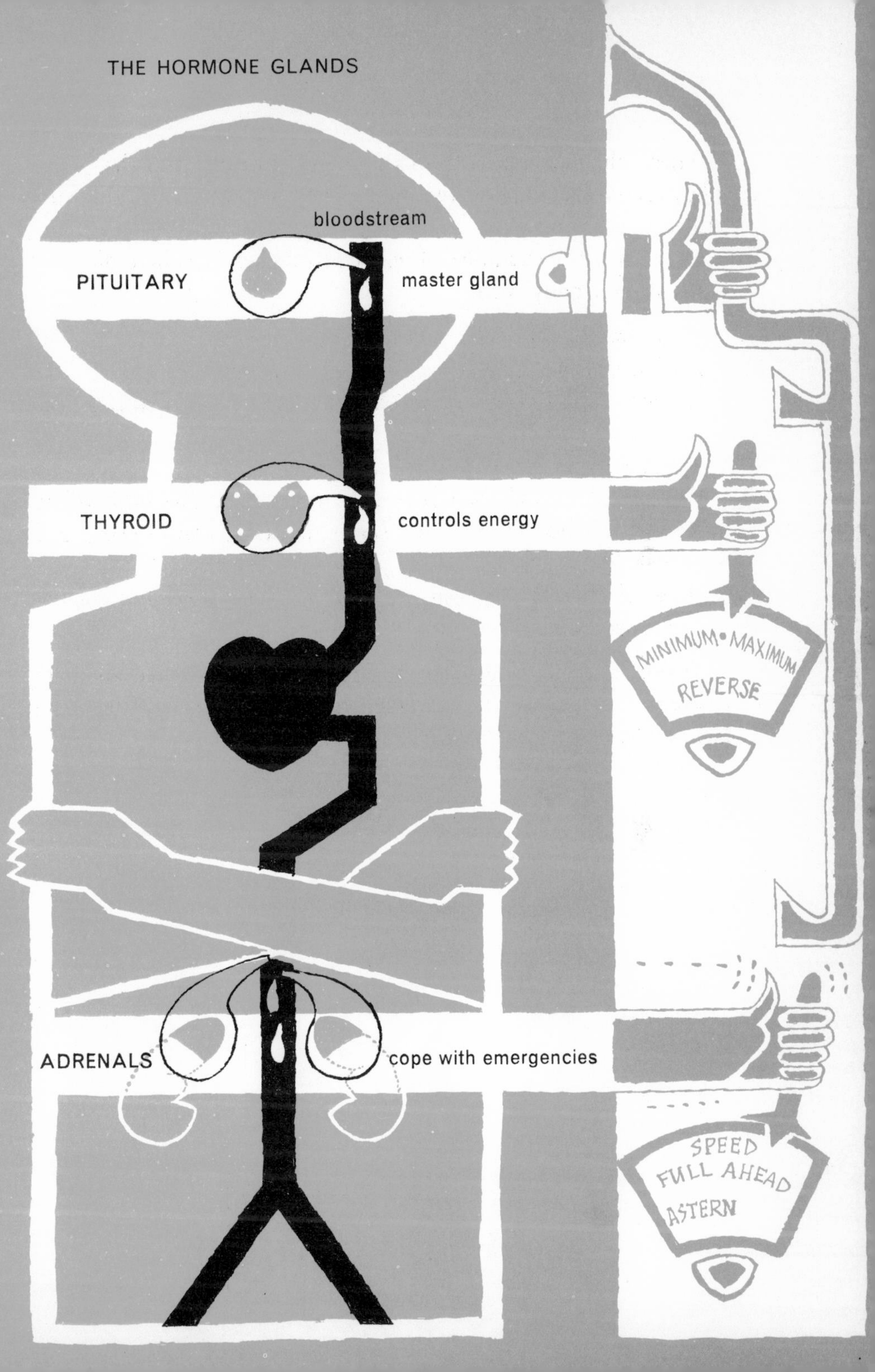

bloodstream

PITUITARY — master gland

THYROID — controls energy

MINIMUM · MAXIMUM
REVERSE

ADRENALS — cope with emergencies

SPEED
FULL AHEAD
ASTERN

These chemicals pass from the glands directly into the blood. They are carried all over the body. They help to control the work of many parts.

Here are a few examples of how control chemicals help different parts of your body work.

A control chemical helps your heart beat strongly.

A control chemical helps your muscles work well.

A control chemical gives you the extra energy you need when you run a race or play a game.

A chemical controls how your bones grow.

A chemical controls how your cells use energy. Too little of this chemical slows you up – in playing, working, and thinking. Too much of this chemical speeds you up, too much so.

A chemical helps you grow into a pretty young woman or a handsome young man.

And you don't have to study to learn how to make all these wonderful chemicals. It is all taken care of for you, by your gland factories.

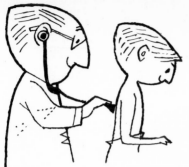

A LIVING PUMP

When you put a watch to your ear, you can hear it go tick-tock, tick-tock. It goes tick-tock without a rest or a stop, as long as it is wound up.

Your heart, too, ticks without a rest or a stop. And it never needs winding.

You can hear a heart tick.

Get a cardboard tube about an inch wide and a foot long.

Put one end of the tube against the chest of a friend. Put your ear to the other end.

Do you hear the sound of the beating heart? It sounds like this: flub, dub; flub, dub.

Next have your friend jump up and down a few times. Then listen to his heart again.

The sounds are the same. But now they are louder and faster. Can you guess why? You will soon find out.

Your heart is about as big as your fist. It is shaped something like a pear turned upside down.

If you put your right fist in the middle of your chest it will be just over your heart. Your fist should point a little to your left.

Why does your heart beat? It is a pump. It pumps blood.

The heart is really a double pump. The right side may be called the lung pump. The left side may be called the body pump.

Each side of the heart, each pump, has two parts. The upper part is like a little bag. The lower part is much larger, and it has a very thick wall. The wall is muscle.

27

Blood is brought by tubes to the bag on the right side of the heart from all parts of the body. When it is filled, it empties the blood into the lower part.

The lower part is the real pump. From the right side of the heart the blood is pumped to the lungs. That is why we call the right side of the heart the lung pump.

The blood is brought back from the lungs by tubes to the little bag on the left side of the heart. When it is filled, it empties the blood into the lower part.

The left side of the heart is the stronger pump. It pumps blood to all parts of the body. That is why we call the left side of the heart the body pump.

Your heart beats about 75 to 80 times a minute while you sit reading this book. That would mean that it beats more than 100,000 times in a day.

Your heart works even harder than this. You know that it beats faster when you play or work, or just move about.

The heart beats faster when you are active because your cell engines need supplies faster. The blood delivers the supplies. And the heart sends it around the body faster.

If you live healthfully, your heart will work well for you for many years, without care or repair. It is a wonderful pump, you must agree.

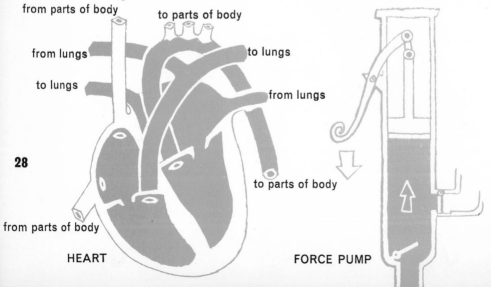

from parts of body   to parts of body

from lungs   to lungs

to lungs   from lungs

to parts of body

from parts of body

HEART   FORCE PUMP

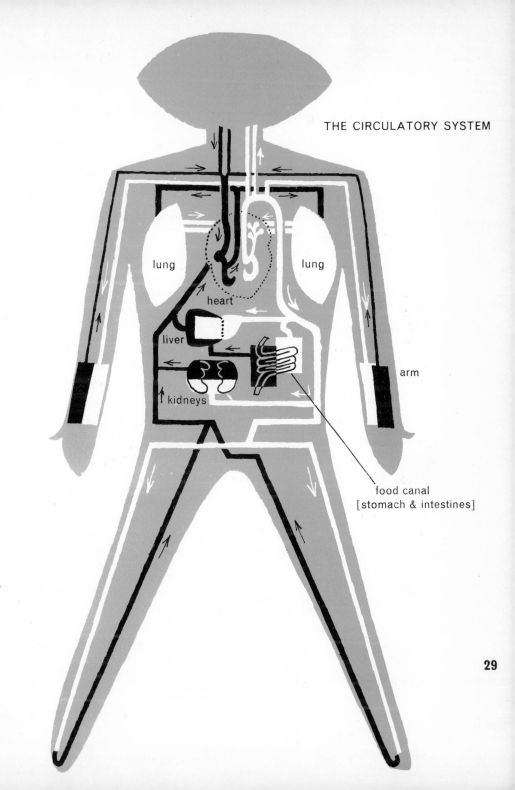

THE CIRCULATORY SYSTEM

lung

lung

heart

liver

arm

kidneys

food canal
[stomach & intestines]

29

red corpuscles

THE BLOOD SUPPLY LINE

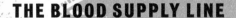
white corpuscles

Your cells work all the time, even while you sleep. Hence the blood must deliver supplies to them day and night.

The blood also takes away wastes from the cells. They would otherwise stop working.

And the blood carries away from the cells some useful products made by the cells, control chemicals, for example.

A little more than half of the blood is water. But not just plain water. There are many chemicals in it. They are mostly those that are being carried to the cells or from them.

There are ever so many tiny red cells floating in the blood. You will find five million or more in one tiny drop of blood.

The red cells take up oxygen in the lungs. They carry it to the body cells.

The oxygen passes from the red cells into the body cells. Carbon dioxide passes from the body cells into the red cells.

The red blood cells then carry the carbon dioxide to the lungs. The lungs get rid of it when you breathe out.

There are also white cells in the blood. They are larger than the red cells. And there are fewer of them, one to every 500 red cells.

The white cells are called "eating cells". They kill germs that may get into the body by eating them.

You know that if you scratch or cut your skin, blood comes out. What prevents all of it from running out of your body? That is taken care of in the blood.

There is a material in the blood which becomes a net of threads when the blood from the cut meets the air. The red and white cells make up the net. The net and the cells make up the clot.

30

This fills the cut and stops the bleeding.

You put a plaster or bandage on the cut to keep the clot in place. When it is dry, it is a scab. Now the cut is well closed. When the cut is healed, the scab drops off.

Bleeding from a large or deep cut does not stop so easily. The flow of blood does not let a clot form in the cut. Such cuts must be treated by a doctor.

As you know, the blood starts its journey round the body from the left side of the heart. It leaves through a tube that is about as wide as your thumb. Branches from this tube go to every part of the body.

HOW THE BLOOD CHANGES AS IT GOES AROUND THE BODY

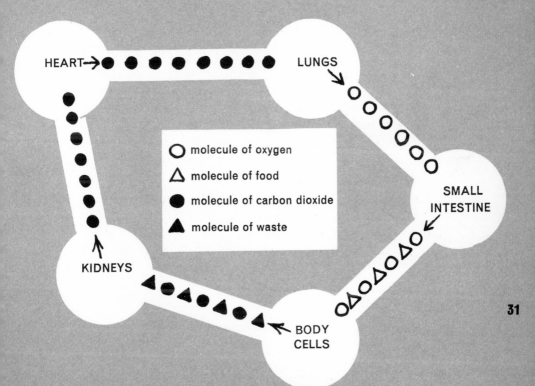

○ molecule of oxygen

△ molecule of food

● molecule of carbon dioxide

▲ molecule of waste

These are your arteries. Arteries carry blood away from the heart.

The smallest arteries are thin as hairs. They branch to make tiny nets around groups of cells. The nets are made up of even finer tubes called capillaries.

On the other side of the net, the hair-like tubes join to make small veins.

Some of the blood oozes out of the tiny tubes of the net. It is then called white blood because it has no red cells in it. The white blood surrounds the net and the cells.

The supplies for the cells leave the blood through the tiny tubes of the net. Materials from the cells are absorbed into the blood through these tubes.

Everything passes through the white blood. That is how it helps in supplying the cells and in getting rid of the wastes from the cells.

The smallest veins join to make larger ones. These join to make still larger ones. The blood is now on the way back to the heart.

Veins carry blood to the heart from all parts of the body.

The white blood is not lost. It is brought back through tubes into a vein. And so all the blood is brought back to the heart.

Each time the heart beats it pumps blood into the arteries. The arteries stretch as the blood is forced into them. This is the pulse.

You can feel your pulse on the inside of your wrist. You can feel it also in your temples, on the sides of your forehead.

It takes much longer to read about the journey of the blood round the body than it really takes. A red blood cell makes a complete journey round the body in half a minute.

small artery   cells   small vein

capillaries

PROTECTING THE INSIDES

An automobile engine gets fouled up when wastes collect in it. Then it loses power, makes funny noises, gets overheated.

The engine can be taken apart and cleaned. Then it works well again.

Your body can also get fouled up with waste. Then you lose energy. You may even overheat. We call it fever.

But the body cannot be taken apart for cleaning. It cleans itself, as it works. Getting rid of body waste is part of living.

You know that food waste is the part of the food that you eat that is not or cannot be changed by your enzymes and digested. The food waste collects in the wide food tube. It stays there twelve or more hours.

While it is there, it begins to decay. Poisons may be made. They may get into the blood and be carried to the cells. That's when you lose energy.

Mothers train children to get rid of such waste by using the toilet at regular times. It is a good habit to keep up all through life.

The cell engines work all the time, as you know. Carbon dioxide gets into the blood. A large amount of carbon dioxide may be a poison.

The harder you play, the more carbon dioxide gets into the blood. But the more carbon dioxide that gets into the blood, the faster you breathe to get rid of it. You don't have to do anything about it. Your brain takes care of your breathing.

An automobile engine wears as it works. Your cell engines wear also. Unlike an auto engine, your cell engines repair themselves, even while they work.

33

The protoplasm breaks down as the cells work. This is what we call wear in the body. The main waste that results from this wear is urea.

Urea is cell waste. It is a body poison.

The urea from the cells passes into the blood. It is carried to the kidneys and the skin.

You have two kidneys, each one about the size of your fist. As the blood flows through your kidneys, they remove urea along with water and some other wastes.

Suppose you eat too much candy at one time. The body gets more sugar than it can use or store at the time. The extra sugar gets into the blood. The kidneys remove it from the body.

The kidneys produce a watery waste. It is mostly water with just a little urea and a few other wastes. It is known as urine.

From the kidney the urine passes to the bladder. As it fills, the pressure reminds one to empty it.

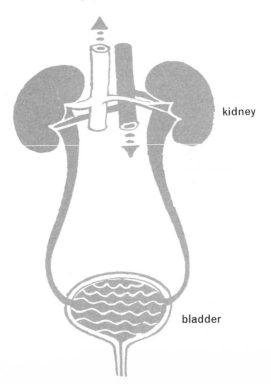

kidney

bladder

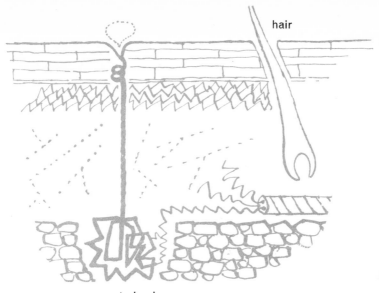

hair

sweat glands

You get rid of some urea through the skin. You do so when you sweat.

You sweat a little all the time. When you play hard you get wet with sweat.

Sweat is mostly water with a very small amount of urea and salt. It comes from millions of tiny sweat glands in the skin. They help the kidneys get rid of urea from the body.

You get thirsty after playing. That is a signal from your throat to replace the water that your body has lost from the kidneys, from the sweat glands, and from the lungs.

You lose about four good sized glasses of water in a day. You replace it by drinking milk and plain water.

The inside of the body must be protected from germs as well as from waste.

Sometimes when you get a small cut, germs may get in through the skin. At once, white blood cells squeeze out of tiny blood tubes that are near the cut. They fight off the germs. You remember that white blood cells eat germs.

Often many white blood cells and germs are killed in the fight. Then pus forms at the cut. It is made up in large part of the killed blood cells and the killed germs.

Sometimes the germs may get into the blood stream. They meet white blood cells. A hot fight takes place, that causes fever. The white blood cells win, as a rule. That is one good reason why we stay healthy.

Sometimes the germs make poisons in the blood. These poisons would harm the cells.

Poisons made by germs are called toxins. The blood is able to make antitoxins. These are chemicals that make the poisons of the germs, the toxins, harmless.

Doctors may help the blood to fight germs by giving you injections. The injection may be an antitoxin that has been made in the blood of some animal. Or it may be a vaccine.

Vaccines are chemicals that cause your blood to make other chemicals that will protect you against certain germs that may get into your blood.

Do you know what injections you have had? Have you had injections to protect you against polio, diphtheria, scarlet fever, some other sickness?

Harmful materials may come from within the body or from the outside. The cells must be protected from wastes that come from within the body and germs that may come from the outside. Then they will work well for you.

THE BODY FRAME

When a house is built, first you see the frame. You can tell the size and shape of the house from its frame.

As soon as the frame is finished, the inside fittings are put in. There are pipes to bring water and to carry away wastes. Other pipes carry heat round the house. Wires are strung for lighting the house. A furnace is put in to supply heat.

Later, each room is fitted out for its work. The kitchens, for example, will have stoves for cooking, sinks for washing and drawing water, maybe a clothes washer, a dish washer and other machines.

The frame of the house supports all the parts that are built into the house.

Your body also has a frame to support all your parts. It is your skeleton.

Your skeleton is made up of more than 200 bones. They are held together by strong bands. Muscles that are fixed to the bones help to hold them together.

A house has posts that hold it up. Your skeleton has a backbone or spine that holds you up straight.

Your backbone is a strong post. But it is not a solid post. It is made up of 26 separate bones placed one on top of the other.

The bones are held together by many strong bands and many small muscles. That is why you can bend forward, or backward, or sideways. And the bones do not slip out of place.

The backbone rests on a strong, bony base called the pelvis. Your hip bones are part of the pelvis. And your legs are joined to your hips.

37

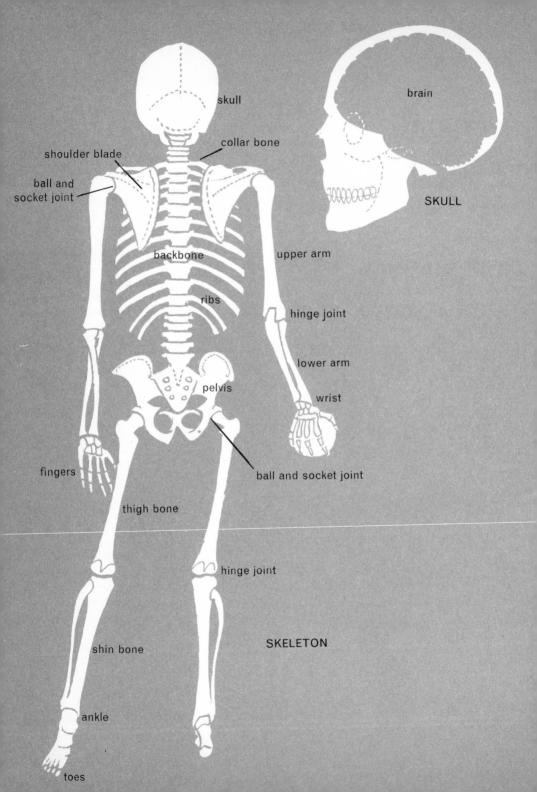

skull

brain

collar bone

shoulder blade

ball and
socket joint

SKULL

backbone

upper arm

ribs

hinge joint

lower arm

pelvis

wrist

fingers

ball and socket joint

thigh bone

hinge joint

shin bone

SKELETON

ankle

toes

Your skull rests on top of the backbone. It is a strong, bony box. It houses the brain. You will learn later why the brain must be so well protected.

So, you see, your head sits on one end of the backbone. You sit on the other end.

Twelve pairs of curved bones, the ribs, are joined to the backbone. The first ten pairs of ribs are joined, also, to the breastbone in the front.

The ribs, together with the backbone and the breastbone, make a sort of basket which houses and protects some of your very important inner parts.

The ribs are also used in breathing. There are many muscles joined to them. When these muscles tighten, they pull up the ribs. This makes your chest larger. Then you draw in air.

When the same muscles slacken, the ribs are lowered. This makes your chest smaller. Then you push air out from your lungs.

Spread your hands on your ribs. Do you feel them as they are raised and lowered? as you breathe?

The collar bones in the front, and the shoulder blades in the back make a kind of collar around the upper part of the ribs. Your arms are joined to these bones.

All the parts of the skeleton that you have just learned about make up the trunk. Your limbs are joined to the trunk.

Your limbs are your arms and your legs. In some ways they are like one another. In other ways they are quite different. They have very different uses.

You stand, run, dance, walk, or jump on your legs. Their bones have to be very strong to support the weight of your body, and to stand up to the pounding they get.

The upper leg bone, the one that is joined to the hip, is your thigh. It is a long, strong, thick bone. The most powerful muscles that move you about are attached to the thigh bone.

39

The lower leg is made up of two long bones. One is thick and strong. This is your shin bone. The other is much thinner. They are joined to the thigh bone at the knee; to the foot at the ankle. And they are joined to one another.

The upper arm, the bone that is joined to the shoulder, is also long, strong and thick. But it is less so than the thigh bone. The strong muscles that are attached to it allow you to lift, pull, and push.

The lower arm is made up of two bones, like the lower leg. One bone is thick, the other thin. They are joined to the upper arm bone at the elbow; to the hand at the wrist. And they are joined to one another.

The fact that your limbs are made up of an upper and a lower part lets you use them so much better. Can you imagine how

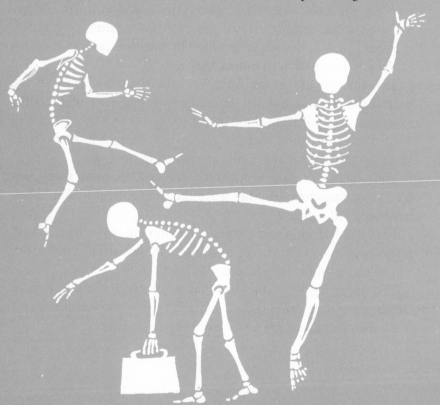

hard it would be to walk or dance if your legs were stiff at the knees? And how could you put a spoon to your mouth if you could not bend your arm at the elbow?

When you stand, walk, run, dance, or jump the whole weight of your body rests on the feet. They are joined to the legs at the ankles.

An ankle is made up seven bones, joined to one another by strong bands. That is why you are able to bend and twist your feet so well.

The strongest and largest of the ankle bones are the heel bones. Just imagine what a pounding they get as you walk on them all day!

The hands are joined to the arms at the wrists. A wrist is made up of eight small bones, joined to one another by strong bands.

Hold one wrist with the fingers of the other hand. Now twist the wrist in every direction. It is because it is made up of the eight small bones that you can twist it in this way.

If you have watched a monkey, as you surely must have, you know that its hands and feet look very much alike. And they can use them in the same ways.

Your hands and feet are alike, in many ways. Thus you have the same number of fingers as you have toes. And a finger has the same number of bones as a toe.

The palm of your hand has the same number of bones as the arch of the foot.

But you use your hands very differently from the way you use your feet. Have you ever tried to walk on your hands or to pick up something with your toes?

All your bones are more or less hollow. They are, none the less, strong. In the hip bones, the breastbone, and the ribs the hollow part is filled with red marrow. This is where the red blood cells are made.

Your body frame is alive. It grows. It can repair itself.

MOVING THE PARTS OF THE BODY

After the frame of a house has been put up, it is covered. The outer cover of a house may be wood, brick, metal, or even glass.

When the house has been covered you can see its real form. And the inside parts are made safe from the weather.

Your body frame is also covered. Your skeleton is covered with muscles.

The bones and muscles together give your body its shape. The muscles that cover the trunk help to keep the parts on the inside safe from harm.

But your muscles also move parts of your body. See how your muscles work when you bend your arm.

Hold your hand on the muscle on the front of your upper arm. Now bend your lower arm.

Do you feel the muscle become tight and short? That is what you call "making a muscle". When a muscle becomes short and tight it pulls a bone.

Next put the same hand on the back of the upper arm. Then make your lower arm straight.

Do you feel the muscle on the back become short and tight? The lower arm is pulled down by this muscle. It doesn't just drop.

The muscles of your arms and legs work in pairs. One muscle of the pair pulls a bone one way. The other muscle of the pair pulls it the other way. When one muscle tightens, the other one slackens.

For most work many muscles are used. For example, when you lift a chair, the muscles of your back and of your legs help the arm muscles.

42

Not all muscles move bones. Muscles open and close your eyes. You use the muscles of your tongue to lick a lollipop. You use the muscles of your lips when you kiss someone.

There are different kinds of muscles on the inside of your body. For example, the walls of your food pipes are mostly muscle. These muscles push the food along through the pipes.

You have some muscles that don't work. They could do so, if you tried hard and often to make them work.

For example, you have muscles on your head, behind your ears, that could wag them, like a puppy does. You could learn to wag your ears, a little.

It is the way that the bones are joined to one another that allows your muscles to move them in the way they do.

When a cowboy swings his rope, his whole arm twists at the shoulder. The arm makes a ball joint with the shoulder.

You can see how such a joint works. Make a tight fist with one hand. Put the fingers of the other hand around it. Then twist the fist in every direction. That is like a ball joint.

Your legs make ball joints with your hip bones. That is why you can walk, run, jump, kick, or dance. But your legs cannot move quite as freely as your arms.

Your knee is a hinge, or swing, joint. This joint is like the hinge by which a door is joined to its frame. The hinge joint lets

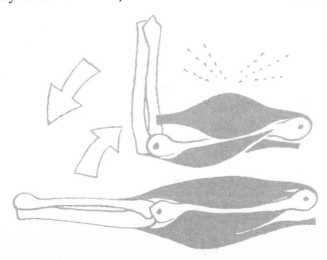

you swing your lower leg up and down. A hinge joint is a swing joint.

Your elbow is also a hinge joint. That is why you can move your lower arm up and down.

But you can also turn and twist your lower arm. The elbow is really a double joint.

The bones of your fingers are joined by hinge joints. That is why you can grab and hold things. See how your fingers work when you hold a ball, or an apple, or a pencil, or a spoon, or a skipping rope.

The bones of your toes are also joined by hinge joints. You can hold some things with your toes. Try to grab a pencil, or a marble. Monkeys can use their toes much better than you can use yours. Their toes are more like fingers.

Muscles and bones work together to do many jobs for the body.

They give your body its shape and form.
They make it possible for you to stand up straight.
They make it possible for you to move things.
They make it possible for you to hold things.
They protect many of your inner parts.

44

THE TEAMS OF THE BODY

Your body works in some ways like a machine. But your body is alive. That makes it very different.

You know that your body is made up of very tiny units called cells, thirty trillion of them. Each one is a working unit.

But the cells do not work by themselves, each one on its own. Cells are organized into working parts.

The working parts of your body are the organs. An organ is made up of very many cells, of several different kinds. They all work together at one special job.

Thus, your eye, heart, liver, kidney, tongue, stomach are organs. How can the work of the body get done by a lot of different organs?

The answer is that the organs work in teams. A team of organs is called a system. All the organs of a system work together at one large job.

For example, the nose, windpipe, and lungs are organs that make up a system. This system supplies fresh air to the body and gets rid of used air.

You have already learned about six body systems. Let's list them.

The system that makes food ready for your cells.
The system that draws fresh air into the body for your cells, and gets rid of the used air from the cells.
The system that brings food and fresh air to the cells and carries away their wastes.
The system that gets rid of the wastes that are carried by the blood.
The system that supports the parts of the body.
The system that moves the parts of the body.

45

THE TEAMS OF THE BODY

From this list you can see that there are many different actions going on in your body at the same time. They are done by many organs, working together in a number of systems.

Wouldn't you think that there should be some way of making sure that all these parts work well together? You have a system that does just that, a control system. You will learn about it soon.

And there is one system more, perhaps the most wonderful of all. It is the system which produces babies.

Most of the organs of the body fit neatly into the trunk. There is room for all. When you have eaten too much, and you feel very full, you may not think so.

The trunk is divided into two parts by a strong muscle. It is the same muscle that helps in breathing.

The upper part of the trunk is the chest. The heart and lungs are in the chest. You know about the bony basket that helps to protect them.

Most of the other organs of the body, except the limbs, are in the lower part of the trunk. It is called the belly or abdomen.

One organ is set apart, in a special, strong housing. It is the brain, which is in the skull of the head.

You should know that this organ controls or manages all the other organs of the body. Some organs it controls directly. It has a hand in controlling other organs. So you see why it has to be made safe by itself in the skull.

It may be very well to learn about your body in parts – cells, organs, systems. But now think of your body as one well-organized, well-run, self-controlled machine. Every little part, every cell, does its share. Then you are in good health.

SENTRIES OF THE BODY

You have a good idea that there are many actions going on in your body at this moment. How does the control team keep the organs working together, in good order?

Your sense organs are the sentries of the control team. They let you know what goes on about you.

Mostly you learn what is happening around you through your eyes. They tell you if it is light or dark, when something is near or far, large or small. Your eyes tell you the size, shape, color and movement of things.

Your eye is like a camera. It has a shutter, a lens, and film.

Your eyelids do the work of the shutter of the camera. On the inside of the eye is a lens. This makes the picture on the film sharp and clear.

You do not have to change films to see, as you must change films in a camera to take many pictures. The film of your eye is called the retina.

The retina receives light signals which come from the object that you are looking at. These light signals are carried to your brain. The brain sees these light signals as a picture.

Your eyes are, indeed, like moving-picture cameras. But you don't need rolls of film to see the moving objects. The light signals that keep coming into the retina are seen in the brain as moving pictures.

You really see in the brain. If the back of your brain were hurt you could not see, even though your eyes were not hurt.

Next to the eyes, the most important sentries of your body are your ears. They pick up sound signals.

The outer ear, the part that you can see and feel, is not, however, the part which lets you hear. You can't see that part.

There is a little bone in the side of your skull. It is shaped like the shell of a snail, about the size of one of your finger nails.

Tiny hairs on the inside of this little bone pick up sound signals. The hairs can tell one sound from another. The sound signals are carried to the brain. That is where you hear.

Taste and smell signals are often mixed up. You can prove that this is so. Try this.

Ask a friend to close his eyes and hold his nose so that he cannot smell. No cheating.

Now put a piece of raw onion on his tongue.

Remove the onion and wipe his tongue with a clean paper tissue.

Next put a piece of raw potato on his tongue.

He will not be able to tell which is which. This is because an onion is smelled, not tasted.

You smell with your nose, of course. There are bundles of hairs inside it with which you smell. They can somehow tell one odor from another.

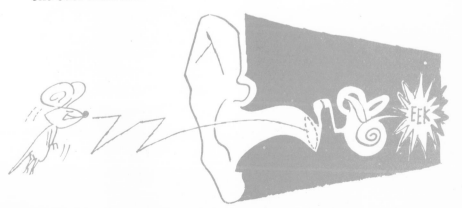

Your tongue can taste sweet or sour, salty or bitter things. A different part of the tongue is used for each kind of taste. You can have fun finding out which part of your tongue tastes each.

Your skin tells you if something is hot or cold, smooth or rough, sharp or dull.

Signals from all the sense organs are carried to your brain.

There are inner senses, too. They report to the brain if the inner organs need attention. Here are a few inner senses that you know well: hunger, thirst, stomach-ache.

Some signals are stored, somehow, in the brain. That is what we call memory. That is how you remember a face, a tune, a taste, these words.

Some signals are passed over in the brain to a part that controls certain muscles or glands. That is why you look up when you hear your name. That is why your mouth waters when you smell something cooking that you like.

Some signals are passed over in the brain to still another part of the brain where you think, and reason things out.

That is how you work out an arithmetical problem after you have seen it, read it, or heard it. That is how you plan and build a project for school.

Your sense organs tell your brain what is going on around you, inside you. Your brain controls what you do as a result of these reports.

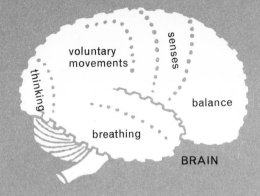

voluntary movements
senses
thinking
balance
breathing
BRAIN

CONTROLLING THE WORK OF THE BODY

Each of us has a will. This means that we can control certain of our actions. For example, you can will to turn the pages of this book when you have read the last words of the last line of a page.

But there are certain actions that you cannot control, at least, not by your will. For example, try to stop the beating of your heart.

Or try to stop breathing. You may hold your breath for a moment. But then you will start to breathe in spite of yourself. And when you play hard you breathe faster without any thought or control on your part.

Your brain is the control center of your body. Those actions that you do because you will to do them are controlled in the forebrain. This is the largest part of the brain and takes up most of the space in your skull.

Make a list of the actions that you control in the forebrain. They would include brushing your teeth in the morning; dressing; using a spoon, a fork, or a knife when you eat; packing your books for school; pedalling your bicycle, and so on.

There are many actions that are controlled in the forebrain that need a lot of attention at first. But as you do them again and again, practice them, they need less and less attention. After a while you do them perfectly without thought or attention.

51

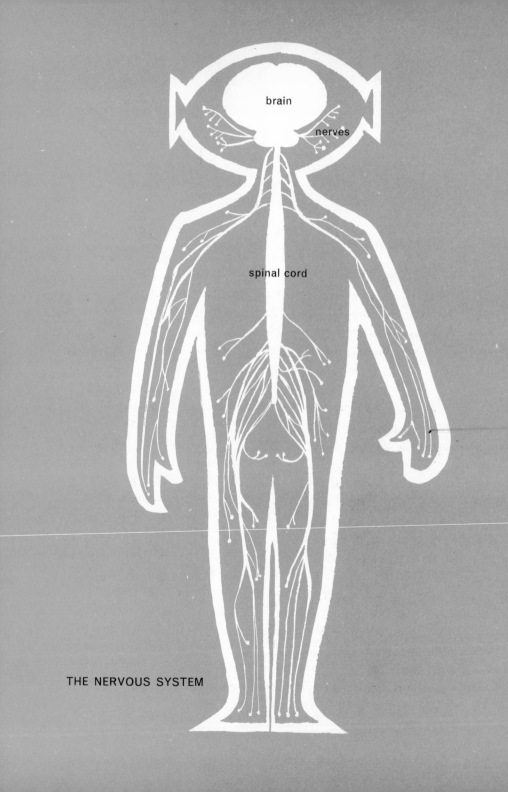

THE NERVOUS SYSTEM

These are habits. This is how you learned to write, table manners, to play the piano, to use a tool, and very many actions that you do every day.

Good habits make everyday work and play so much easier.

If you think of it, standing, walking, or running on two feet without flopping over is quite a trick. Many muscles must be balanced to keep you up. They are controlled in the hindbrain, without any attention from you.

Still another part of the brain is the center for controlling breathing, the movements in the food tubes, sneezing, coughing, and yawning. Can you will to control any of these actions? Try to stop them!

And there are still other control centers. For example, if you touch something hot, you pull your hand away even before you feel the heat. You don't stop to think whether you should or should not do so.

The control center for many such actions is in the spinal cord. This is a bundle of nerves, like a rope. It starts in your brain and runs through your backbone, almost to the end.

It works like a chain of stations that control certain local actions. The spinal cord would be the center that controls your raising your leg suddenly when you step on a tack.

Many of your inner organs, such as the stomach and kidneys have their own control centers.

When these organs work well, they do so without any thought or attention from you. That is a good thing, too! If you had to pay attention to their working, you would have little time or thought for anything else.

But when things really go wrong in any part of the body a message is sent to the brain, the forebrain, for action. That is the center where memory, thought, and reason control action.

Signals from sense organs are carried to control centers by nerves. Signals from control centers to working organs, such as muscles and glands, are carried by other nerves. Nerves work like the wires that carry electricity in your homes.

Nerves reach out to every part of the body. In this way signals from every organ reach control centers. And signals from control centers reach every organ.

The many nerves that go to and from the brain join to make a thick cord, the spinal cord. You already know that it is a chain of stations that control some local actions.

All but a few signals to and from the brain pass through the spinal cord. A few organs, mostly in the head, are connected directly to the brain. For example, the eye, ear, nose, and throat are connected in this way.

Making a phone call is something like the working of your control system.

When you dial a number, you send signals through a wire. The dial is like a sense organ. The wire from the telephone carries the signals to a cable.

The cable is like the spinal cord. It brings the signals to a switchboard. The switchboard is the control center. Here the incoming signals are switched. That is, they are passed over to a place from which signals are sent out.

A signal goes out from the switchboard through a cable. A wire from the cable goes to the telephone that you are calling. A bell rings.

If you think a telephone system is wonderful, how much more wonderful is your control system. It can do so much more, so much better. It is alive.

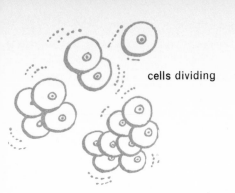
cells dividing

LIVING IS GROWING

Would you like to have your picture in this book? Well, here it is. This is what you really looked like, at one time.

You were very much smaller. You were the size of a tiny dot.

You have grown a lot. You started life as a single cell. Now you are made up of thirty trillion cells.

Growth means adding more cells. It means, also, that cells get larger. For example, you haven't added any muscle or nerve cells since you were born. But these cells have grown larger.

More cells and larger cells means adding protoplasm. A cell takes in food from the blood. It changes these food stuffs into protoplasm. In this way a cell gets larger.

When each kind of cell reaches the limit of its growth, it divides into two parts. It becomes two cells.

A cell doesn't just break into two pieces. Each time a cell becomes two, it does so in exactly the same way.

This is called cell division.

You are made up of different kinds of cells. You think with brain cells. You move your arms with muscle cells. Gland cells make chemicals.

Very early in your growth, before you were born, some cells became different from other cells. Each kind became fitted for one special kind of work. Then each kind made more like itself, by cell division.

55

This growth from one kind to many cells of different kinds follows a plan. But we do not know how this plan is controlled in the body.

Since you were born, you grew faster during your first year. Many mothers measure the child's growth every week during this year. Do you still have your record of growth?

You should get ready for a great burst in growth. It begins about the age of ten. This is the time when your parents are likely to say, "He (she) is shooting up like a bean stalk."

You will feel clumsy during this growing time. Your feet may get in your way, and in other people's way. You will grow out of your clothes quickly.

Your arms and legs will grow faster than the rest of you. That's how we grow. The body, at first, grows faster than the head. The arms and legs grow faster than the body.

But it all balances out. The body growth catches up with the growth of the arms and the legs. And the head does not appear to be too large for the body.

Girls grow faster than boys of the same age, at this time. But the boys soon catch up.

Boys keep on growing until they are about twenty-one years old. Girls grow very little after the age of eighteen.

Girls and boys want to know how tall they will grow. That depends, in the first place, on their parents, or maybe their grandparents.

The limit to which you will grow is passed on to you by your mother and father. There is something in the cell from which you start which controls growth.

To reach your limit of growth you will need enough of the right kinds of foods. You know what they are.

You will need, also, enough of a control chemical made in the brain by the "master" gland. It makes a chemical that controls the growth of the bones of the face, the arms, and the legs.

A circus giant got too much of this chemical while he was growing up. A circus midget got too little. You grow up right when you get just enough.

However, you do not stop growing altogether when you reach the limit of your growth in height.

As you play or work, your cells wear out. The worn cells are replaced. This is done, as you know, by cell division. In this way other cells replace the worn ones.

This is called repair. Your body repairs itself by the growth of new cells.

So long as one lives, one grows. Growing is needed for living.

A NEW LIFE IS BORN

I think your dad would like this idea. When his car gets old, he takes a very small part, say a bolt or a nut, from it. He gives it tender, loving care. After a time it grows into a nice new car to replace the old one.

Sounds silly, doesn't it. Yet the story of the birth and growth of a baby is something like that.

A tiny bit of a parent, smaller than a tiny dot, grows to become first a baby, then a child, then a boy or a girl, and at last a man or a woman. A child is born to take the parents' place, one day.

It starts in the mother. She produces eggs, one at a time. They are very tiny.

When you think of an egg, you may have in mind a chicken egg. That is very large.

The reason for this is that the mother hen stores a lot of food in the egg for the growing young chick. It uses this food for growth until it is ready to hatch.

The human egg is very tiny because the growing young one is fed from the blood of the mother until it is born.

A baby is the child of the father as well as of the mother. The father adds something to the mother's egg. He adds a sperm cell. The sperm cell and the egg cell become one inside the mother.

Then the egg begins to divide. First there are two cells, then four, then many, many more. You know that when the baby is born the one cell will have become trillions of cells.

The growth of the baby follows a plan. How this plan is controlled in the body so that a normal baby is born, is one of the greatest mysteries of life.

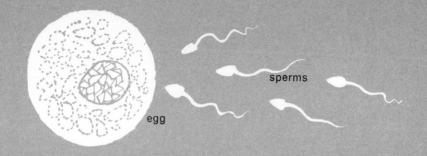

egg

sperms

The young one develops within the mother. It is joined to her by a cord.

Blood tubes from the developing young one run through this cord. The blood from these tubes runs close to the blood tubes of the mother.

Food and oxygen pass from the mother's blood into that of the young one. Waste passes from the blood of the young one into the mother's blood. She gets rid of it, along with her own wastes.

It will take nine months for the baby to grow in the mother, before it is ready to leave the mother.

By the end of the first month the young one is about the size of a grain of rice, about one quarter of an inch. The beginning of some organs can be seen.

At the end of two months, the young one has developed a head, eyes, ears, arms, and legs. It has inner organs, too, of course. But none of the organs are well developed. And the young one doesn't look anything like a baby.

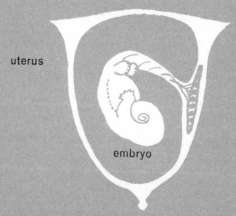

uterus

embryo

59

By the end of the fourth month we may be sure that it is a baby that is growing. It begins to move. It is about seven inches long. But it isn't at all pretty.

After the fourth month it is a matter of time while the organs grow larger.

By the end of the ninth month the baby is ready to leave the mother's body. It has been fed, kept warm, and protected within the mother's body.

The baby comes out into the world in which it will live. The cord that held it to the mother is cut. The baby is then on its own, but not altogether.

The newborn baby must start to breathe, to feed itself, to digest the food it eats, to get rid of waste.

The baby gasps. This fills its lungs with air and it starts to breathe.

The baby's lips make a sucking sound. It will know how to take in food.

Still the newborn baby will need help. It will have to be fed, bathed, kept warm.

Its bones are too soft to support its body, its muscles too weak to support it. Another year or more will pass before the baby will take its first step.

Babies have so much to learn. They start to do so almost from the moment of birth.

Watch a baby as it moves its eyes about, taking everything in. Watch it as it touches everything it can lay its hands on. Watch it as it takes things into its mouth.

The baby is learning by seeing, feeling, and tasting.

And babies must be loved. They somehow know when they are. Babies that are loved behave better, grow up healthier.

You are the kind of boy or girl that you are because of the tender, loving care you got as a baby.

Babies grow up to be boys and girls like you. Now would you like to see the greatest of all wonders? Look in a mirror.

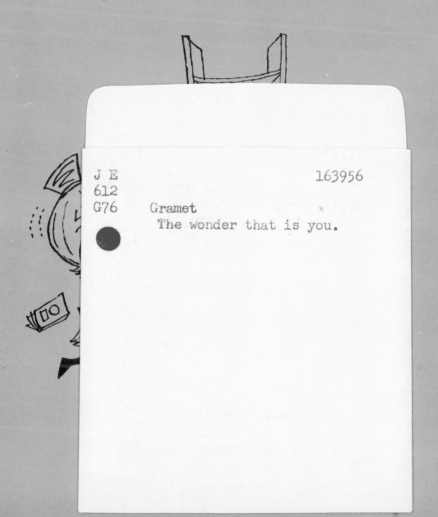